EXCELLING IN
BASEBALL

By Shirley Duke

ReferencePoint
Press®

San Diego, CA

© 2020 ReferencePoint Press, Inc.
Printed in the United States

For more information, contact:
ReferencePoint Press, Inc.
PO Box 27779
San Diego, CA 92198
www.ReferencePointPress.com

LIBRARY OF CONGRESS CATALOGING-IN-PUBLICATION DATA

Names: Duke, Shirley Smith, author.
Title: Excelling in baseball / by Shirley Duke.
Description: San Diego, California : ReferencePoint Press, Inc., [2020] |
    Series: Teen Guide to Sports | Audience: Grades: 9 to 12. | Includes
    bibliographical references and index.
Identifiers: LCCN 2019005374 (print) | LCCN 2019009880 (ebook) | ISBN
    9781682826966 (ebook) | ISBN 9781682826959 (hardcover)
Subjects: LCSH: Baseball--Training--Juvenile literature. | Baseball
    players--Health and hygiene--Juvenile literature. | Baseball
    players--United States--Conduct of life--Juvenile literature. | Baseball
    players--Vocational guidance--United States--Juvenile literature. | Major
    League Baseball--Juvenile literature.
Classification: LCC GV867.5 (ebook) | LCC GV867.5 .D85 2020 (print) | DDC
    796.357--dc23
LC record available at https://lccn.loc.gov/2019005374

CONTENTS

BECOMING
THE BEST

In the 2009 Major League Baseball (MLB) draft, most teams passed on Mike Trout. In the future, he would become an American League (AL) Most Valuable Player (MVP). But many team managers and scouts believed Trout wasn't what they needed. Trout's high school coach explained his possible weaknesses. "He hadn't played the outfield for very long; he was a shortstop and pitcher his whole life," Coach Roy Hallenbeck said. "We moved him to the outfield his senior year, so he had maybe thirty games under his belt as an outfielder. His swing was a little raw; very aggressive and very strong, but a little raw, so there were questions about whether or not that would clean up and if he could hit."[1] Hallenbeck acknowledged his player's athleticism and saw him continually getting better, but he didn't blame the teams that passed him over. He agreed that he wouldn't have chosen him early in the draft either.

Ten years later, Mike Trout was arguably the best player in MLB. He has collected seven All-Star selections, two AL MVPs, and an

Mike Trout became one of the top players in professional baseball. But few people saw his potential in the beginning.

AL Rookie of the Year Award, among numerous other accolades. In hindsight, it's hard to believe that so many teams passed him over for other, seemingly more talented players. He was finally chosen by the Los Angeles Angels with the twenty-fifth pick. The Angels' scouting director at the time said, "He shouldn't have been there at twenty-five, but we'll take him."[2]

It could have been easy for Trout to doubt himself after being passed on by most teams in MLB. Being a later pick didn't deter him, however. Trout says, "A lot of people doubted me. I just try to prove them wrong each and every day."[3] In 2011, he won Minor League Player of the Year while playing for the Angels' AA minor league team in Arkansas. And he kept on going, working to improve. By 2012 he was an MLB star. His statistics and awards over his career have shown his ability and determination to get better. He isn't satisfied with being great at one or two skills but instead works continually to get better at every part of his game. "I put my mind into something," Trout said, "and the results are there."[4] Trout's example of believing in himself and working to improve shows how a talented player can become great.

CHARACTERISTICS OF SUCCESSFUL PLAYERS

Successful players can hit, catch, and throw much better than the average player, but it's not just the above-average physicality and talent that makes them great. Baseball also requires a mental edge. Baseball players at the highest levels are able to coordinate their minds and bodies. Quick reactions, a strong focus, and excellent vision are necessary for success. Columbia University conducted studies on the famous Babe Ruth, showing he reacted much more quickly to visual and auditory cues than the average person. The study also noted that his hand-eye coordination was better than

Baseball features long periods of waiting, punctuated by moments of athleticism. Playing the game requires both physical ability and mental focus.

98.8 percent of people. These traits led to the ability to hit fastballs and not only see the spin on a curveball but also make contact with it.

Baseball is a high-speed game mixed with moments of inactivity. That's why focus is so important. Focus on the game requires remaining mentally ready at all times, even during the slow moments. Mental preparation allows players to act when the speed of play requires it. This focus lets players drown out everything beyond the game. Retired eleven-time all-star and 1986 AL MVP pitcher Roger Clemens once said when he focused, all he saw was the catcher, but

Pitching can take a significant toll on a player's body. Physical training mixed with mental discipline can help reduce the damage.

when he lost focus, he was "seeing the crowd, not just the catcher."[5] Performances in baseball can go up and down, but the best players must remain at an even emotional attitude throughout the season. "I'm not a guy that shows a lot of emotion while I'm playing," says Houston Astros second baseman José Altuve.[6]

Mental toughness includes the ability to rebound from failure while remaining under emotional control. This, coupled with a strong desire to make something happen, leads to success on the field. When a hitter's batting average is over .300, it's considered good.

"When I joined an all-boys baseball team, my mom wasn't too happy. I proved to her (and to me) that I could do anything I set my mind to."[7]

– Mo'ne Davis, former Little League star

That means that even a good hitter fails about seven out of ten times. Remaining confident is a valuable tool for a baseball player. Pitcher Mo'ne Davis, the first girl to pitch a shutout in the Little League World Series, says, "When I joined an all-boys baseball team, my mom wasn't too happy. I proved to her (and to me) that I could do anything I set my mind to."[7]

Getting the competitive edge in a sport requires determination, hard work, and a mindset of constant improvement. These factors are seen in the most successful baseball players. The good news is that anyone can develop these attributes.

CHAPTER ONE

WHAT DOES IT TAKE TO
MAKE THE TEAM?

Setting goals can help a player make the team. A good goal is a concrete achievement that is realistic to reach. Players need a plan on how to get there. They need to know what areas need to improve to make that goal happen. In 2018, Mike Trout set a goal of improving his defense. One of the ways he worked to achieve that was by taking a close look at his mechanics. Trout said, "What we've been working on is my pre-set. I'm already down when the pitch is out of the hand. I'm trying to get down as soon as contact happens so I can make that first jump, as opposed to sitting there for like a half-second, flat-footed."[8] This increased reaction speed pays off in center field. Trout also worked to improve by regularly tracking balls off the bat during batting practice in spring training.

CREATING GOALS THROUGH SELF-ASSESSMENT

When a player identifies a need, he can formulate a way to improve his play by breaking the problem down and devising steps to address it. Trout's effort paid off. He became the only regular player at center field not to commit an error in 2018. He saved seven defensive runs and had more putouts than most players at his position.

At any level of play, a coach can help players plan ways to achieve their short-term and long-term goals. Peers can help players remain motivated as they strive to achieve those goals together.

A player needs to know his own strengths and weaknesses. To succeed, players must begin the off-season with a realistic idea of their strengths and weaknesses. They can talk with their coach to identify specific areas to focus on, and then they can set goals that address ways to improve. All off-season work should directly improve performance on the field.

For batting, a player should try to hit to his own strengths and recognize what needs work. Players who hit based on their individual strengths improve the possibility of making the team. Houston Astros second baseman José Altuve says, "I just try to make contact with the ball. It's obvious that I like to swing the bat. I'm not thinking of taking a lot of pitches.”[9] Players like Altuve can swing for contact and get on base more than power hitters.

Besides personal goals, players have team goals. Seattle Mariners outfielder Mitch Haniger said, “Our mindset is just trying to get to the playoffs.”[10] The key to reaching goals is to set achievable ones. San Francisco Giants third baseman Evan Longoria says, “I like to set realistic goals for myself, not outrageous ones.”[11] Houston Astros pitcher Justin Verlander says, “I don't think anybody's goal is to be mediocre. I think everybody should want to be the best. I've always felt that way. I want to be at the best at everything I do.”[12] The first goal in baseball is making the team. At any level, making the team allows players to take the next step in a baseball career. And players must bring their best to tryouts.

OFF-SEASON TRAINING FOR IMPROVEMENT

An athlete must be in the best physical condition possible before trying out, and off-season training helps with this. The off-season is longer than the usual baseball season, so it makes sense for a player to use this time to find ways to improve. Any player can improve on his or her natural abilities and skills during the off-season. The areas a player targets can be anything from hitting, glove work, and tracking the ball to simple strength and conditioning. And a player can target more than one area.

Practices are reduced during the off-season. This is the time for heavy lifting for strength training. Focusing on correct form and flexibility are key to good, safe workouts. Preseason workouts might begin two or three months before the games start. Common drills include a running program for conditioning, a workout plan for strengthening muscles, and hitting and pitching activities.

Pitchers need to rest their throwing arm for several months, but they can continue the other workouts, along with plenty of running. Once the rest period is over, pitchers often throw an extended bullpen session once a week, especially if they aren't pitching in games. Many players and coaches recommend youth pitchers play a different position in summer leagues to rest their arm. Pitching year round can lead to elbow injuries or a player burning out.

Players should include stretching and agility exercises in their workouts at least once or twice a week. Band resistance training is important. It allows developing players to work their muscles without bulking up. Overly built-up muscles can hinder swinging ability and agility. Muscles are important for baseball power, but they must be developed correctly with proper training. Frequent batting practice is important to maintain mechanics and skills. This can be done using soft toss, a pitching machine, or having someone throw pitches.

During tryouts, coaches look for athleticism and physically strong players. Arm strength comes from quality upper-body workouts. Push-ups on a medicine ball can help build up these muscles. Angels first baseman and designated hitter Albert Pujols says, "In regards to core training, I try to incorporate the medicine ball whenever possible. As a baseball player, there is a lot of twisting and turning that I will do. Keeping my abs strong is as important as anything else."[13] Speed comes from lower-body strength. Training using dumbbells to perform one-legged squats helps build up the lower body and increase speed. Sprints also help with speed. Players do uphill and downhill sprints or push weighted sleds to get faster too.

Running on hills can build both stamina and speed. Improvements in these areas help players stay fresh in long games and dash between bases as fast as possible.

Balance and core workouts can improve players' hitting. Exercises that help in these areas include half-kneeling cable chops and leg and arm rows. Half-kneeling cable chops use a rope or stirrup handle attached to a cable stack. Start by kneeling on the leg away from the stack. Using both hands, pull the grip across the body, starting at just above the shoulder. Pull it on a diagonal path across the body. The movement is finished at hip level. Then, return to the starting position. This helps with rotational speed and batting power.

For single-leg arm rows, players hold a kettlebell in the right hand. Players balance on the right leg with the core held tight. They lean forward and balance by keeping the left leg straight with the back. With the left leg and back parallel to the ground and the right arm holding the kettlebell below their torso, players then perform a row.

This is done by pulling the
kettlebell to the chest. Players
can choose to perform one
row per repetition or perform all
the rows before returning back
to the start. These help with
balance and core strength. To
improve the power in a player's

swing, lower-body rotation training can improve bat speed. Veteran
first baseman Adrian Gonzalez says, "Just hit off the tee. It's the most
underrated thing you can do, and it's the best thing you can do to
improve your swing."[14]

BUILDING MORE STRENGTH AND SPEED

Strength translates to speed, so players need to follow a specific
program designed for their needs and position. Strength building
includes deadlifts, squats, presses, and motions for increasing pulling
power. Players should consult with their trainers before beginning a
strenuous off-season workout program. Younger players should talk
with their doctor and parents before starting a weightlifting regimen.
Some strength training exercises, when done without the proper
form, can cause injuries. All players should know the correct form and
practice it without weights before increasing weight.

Off-season training is a time for low reps and high intensity
workouts. Younger players focus on posterior chain strength,
which includes all the muscles of the upper back and down to the
glutes and hamstrings. These muscles provide explosiveness in
other movements. Summer training also addresses developing the
upper body for older players. Next, players can add explosive lifts

Baseball skills are important, but so is building up strength and speed in the gym. Gyms provide a place to execute precise training plans using both resistance and cardio equipment.

at 60 to 85 percent of their one-repetition maximum and alternate with weighted jumps. These sets combine complex motion with strength building.

Drills to work on speed have to reflect baseball's requirements. Baseball requires taking off from a still position, and players need quick feet to do this. Sprinting lines is a way to improve footwork and speed. Players can develop endurance and practice quick changes in direction. Players start from a set line and sprint ninety feet (27 m) to a second line, then turn and sprint back to the first line. Continue this for eight consecutive sets or sixteen sprints. Time the sprints. Record the time and work to lower it during the next workout. Starting in a side shuffle and moving to a sprint helps players work sprints into their workout while introducing lateral movement, which helps with fielding.

Medicine ball throws improve strength using rotations and slams. This works the core muscles around the trunk of the body. Kettlebell swings develop strength in the player's hips. As the off-season progresses, strength exercises should shift to sprints and change-of-direction drills. During preseason, players should focus on using the increased strength they have developed to create speed and endurance. Plyometrics, or exercises that include rapid stretching and contractions of muscles, should be a large part of training during the preseason.

Plyometric training makes muscles contract with full force. This is called muscle fiber recruitment. Jump squats are one example. These and other vertical exercises use the muscles necessary for powerful motion. Other exercises for speed and agility include jumping lunges, broad jumps, lateral jumps, and mountain climbers.

To strengthen rotator cuff muscles, which make the throwing motion possible, players should perform lateral raises. These can be performed with a cable stack or dumbbell. With a dumbbell the player lies on his left side, and his right elbow is kept tight against his side. The dumbbell should be held directly in front of him, with his right hand held so that his arm is parallel to the ground. The weight is rotated upward to the end of the range of motion. Additionally, he can start with the weight against his stomach and begin the lift with the arm perpendicular to the ground and finish with the arm parallel to the ground. This exercise uses the same muscles as throwing, so it should only be done in the off-season when those muscles are less likely to be fatigued.

Kettlebells can be useful components of strength training workouts. Building strength can give baseball players an edge when moving and throwing on the field.

One of the most important parts of off-season training is taking a break. Rest and relaxation during the off-season are crucial for body and mind to recover. They refresh a player so he can be ready for the new season.

GOOD PRACTICES

Working out with a partner or trainer can keep players safe in case they need help and makes sure players use correct form. Many exercises can lead to injury if done incorrectly. Back squats develop lower body strength and power, but they also rotate the shoulder and prevent control of the joint there. This exercise, especially with a heavy weight, can injure the shoulder. Switching to a front squat, using kettlebells for a goblet squat, or using a safety bar can prevent injuries while players maintain most of the benefits of the back squat.

The overhead press is another injury-prone exercise. Younger athletes or those with shoulder injuries may want to substitute this lift with a more stable exercise. Young shoulders don't have the mobility needed or a stable enough torso to do this one safely. Overhead exercises can be done, but players should use light loads for the lift. Performing the lift while seated requires less stability too. Other exercises can help with the correct form for lifts. The kneeling or standing landmine press is a good substitute for the overhead press. It controls the back muscles and prevents full shoulder flexion. The landmine press is performed by using a landmine device or placing a barbell in the corner. Move into a half-kneeling stance in front of the barbell. The knee on the same side as the shoulder doing the exercise should be the one on the ground. Hold the end of the barbell at shoulder height. Press up until the arm is fully extended. The arm should never move directly over the shoulder during the press but should stay in front of the body.

Improper mechanics, overwork, and the kinds of pitches thrown all can make pitchers susceptible to injury. Pitching requires being on line with the front foot and not bringing the throwing arm across the body. Other issues involve not turning over the arm and hand during the throw, the height of the pitching elbow relative to the shoulder, and hip torque during the throw.

BASEBALL SKILLS

In addition to strength, conditioning, and flexibility, players must work on skills specific to the sport of baseball. They should know the details of how to play the game, where they are supposed to be, and what to do. For example, middle infielders should know how to turn a double play. Outfielders are responsible for throwing to the cutoff player and getting the ball to the infield quickly. First and third base players must know when to throw or hold on to the ball and how to cover the baseline.

The five tools, a term used frequently for evaluating baseball players, are the skills needed to excel in baseball. The five tools are hitting for power, contact hitting and consistency, speed, fielding ability, and arm strength. These tools gauge an athlete's overall athleticism and ability. Not everyone who plays baseball excels at all five. The players who do have the potential to become superstars.

THE FIVE TOOLS

Power means how far the player can hit the baseball. Contact hitting has multiple components, including how often a player gets on base. It refers to how often the player makes good contact, avoids hitting fly balls that can be easily caught, and hitting to the whole field. Speed refers to the quickness with which a player can run the bases after making contact with the ball, including how fast the batter leaves the batter's box. Fielding ability has to do with a player's hands, skills in catching the ball, tracking ability, and consistency. Arm strength is the player's raw power in throwing the ball fast and far. For players attempting to make a team, working on improving the five tools helps them improve their chances of making the team. Although few players are elite at all five, any player can improve on their natural ability in all five categories.

However, the five tools aren't a complete measure of talent. Pitch recognition and plate discipline also play a part in predicting excellence in a player. Being able to see the ball and identify the pitch

Andrew McCutchen is widely considered a five-tool player. He has been playing in MLB since 2009.

and spin are critical skills of successful batting. Focus is needed to see the ball, along with good hitting mechanics. Seeing the ball is a skill, and there are drills that can improve how well players see the ball. Visualization drills help batters practice this.

A player can simply watch pitchers work in the bullpens. He can practice hitting against pitching machines set to a higher speed. He can use hitting drills with a smaller-sized ball to improve eye focus. Batters can practice hitting at different distances. There's even a computer game that allows players to identify real pitches from the batter's point of view.

Once a batter has improved his recognition, the next step is being disciplined with this information at the plate. Plate discipline involves the statistics of how often a hitter swings the bat and makes contact with certain kinds of pitches or how often the opposing pitcher causes the batter to swing or connect with specific pitches. Hitters must understand what they are trying to do and go to the plate with a plan for hitting against each particular pitcher. Patience is important. Batters need to wait for the pitch they want and then swing well. Hitters need good mechanics. They need knowledge of what pitch they hit best, the strike zone location of their pitch, and how to work the pitch count. Working these into an off-season program will help all batters improve.

DRILLS FOR TEAM SKILLS

Improving individual skills is valuable, but players need to include drills that will be helpful for team play too. Throwing shows coaches a player's arm strength, so daily throwing is valuable for building up the muscle strength necessary to play baseball. Throwing can be done with as few as two players. The drill around the horn, in which players throw the ball to each other in a set pattern in the infield, improves important infield throws. Another good team throwing drill is called four corners. Players throw the ball around the base path as fast as possible. This helps improve accuracy, arm strength, and footwork.

Beyond drills, catchers should work on throwing to second base. This will help them pick off runners trying to steal a base. Second basemen and shortstops should practice catching runners who are trying to steal second base, picking off players who are leading off, and working together on double plays. Those who play first or third base need to practice throwing to the catcher, throwing across the

Trapping grounders and quickly throwing the ball is critical. Repeated practice can help players hone this skill.

infield, and picking off players who are trying to steal or lead off a base. Hitting the cutoff player is another skill for outfielders. Outfielders work on their crow-hop to increase their momentum for the throw to home. This small jump, done as part of the throwing motion, maximizes distance. The cutoff players should practice catching and quickly throwing to a base or home plate. Cutoff players are usually second base and shortstop. Drills for practicing quick fielding reactions include catching line drives and grounders.

Batting drills require players to hit to different areas of the outfield or infield. This includes bunting too. Players need to be able to hit gaps in the outfield, adjust to whatever pitch is thrown and make contact with it, and bunt efficiently if the coach calls for it.

BASEBALL CAMPS

Players looking to improve their baseball skills can attend baseball camps where they can hone their fielding, batting, and throwing skills. Often, high school coaches hold summer baseball camps. Players can check with coaches to find a locally held camp. Many universities and colleges also hold camps.

Baseball camps typically focus on hitting, throwing, fielding, speed, and agility. The camps teach fundamentals and advanced skills, and they are open to all ages. Players receive intensive instruction and work on skills and confidence. These skills include the mechanics of hitting, mental preparation, situational hitting, base running, infield or outfield play, proper mechanics, and hand-eye coordination drills. Pitching at these camps often includes daily pitching and working on mechanics, delivery, different pitches, and grips for the baseball. Catchers learn to receive balls, to block them, and to improve throwing skills. However, some baseball camps can be costly. Spending time investigating local camps can help players locate ones with a lower cost.

TRAVEL TEAMS

Some players try out for travel or showcase teams. These teams can be more competitive than their high school teams. Often, travel teams provide a place for players hoping to push themselves to the next level. Their tryouts are similar to those for high school teams.

Mo'ne Davis has been one of the most high-profile female baseball players. She was the first African American girl to play in the Little League World Series.

Travel teams are available for girls in certain areas too. Some girls do play on boys' baseball teams, but it is relatively rare.

Fewer opportunities present themselves for girls, but a nonprofit group called Baseball for All has begun to improve that issue. It advocates for girls' baseball teams around the country. Some all-girls travel teams already exist. The Boston Slammers travel team is made up of more than thirty girls ages nine to eighteen. The team works with Jamaica Plain Regan Youth League to play organized baseball. DC Girls Baseball is based in Washington, DC. This organization provides a chance for girls to play in leagues around the city and to travel locally and regionally to compete. Each year, the organization adds

BRYCE HARPER COULDN'T WAIT

Bryce Harper dominated his high school team for two years, making the cover of *Sports Illustrated* at sixteen years old. The talented Harper obtained his GED and enrolled in a Nevada junior college to be eligible for the 2010 MLB draft. He wanted a greater challenge. "High school was a great experience for two years. I loved it," Harper said. "I just want to get out of there where I'm getting walked forty, fifty times a year."

Harper played on travel teams in high school but in 2008 participated in the Area Code Games, a national tournament. The games got him noticed for his batting skills and his attitude. One scouting director commented that Harper was out there to win and played baseball in an old-school way.

The Washington Nationals selected the seventeen-year-old Harper as their number one choice in the 2010 draft. He rose quickly through the minors and made his major league start at nineteen years old. He hit twenty-two home runs in his first season.

Quoted in Keith Law, "Harper Looking for a Challenge," ESPN, June 24, 2009. www.espn.com.

more teams. International teams field baseball teams for girls, and the Women's Baseball World Cup team holds tryouts every year. The tryouts are held after the Women's National Open, another women's baseball competition.

THE DRIVE TO SUCCEED

A player's awareness of his own game, not comparing himself with other players, makes him better. Improvement is in the individual player's hands. The important focus is whether the player is better than the day before. The best players have an internal drive to succeed and get better. Good players hold themselves to a high standard and judge their performance based on their expectations for themselves. But in order to do this, players must be aware of their strengths and weaknesses.

Being competitive is another quality coaches look for in a player. Being competitive pushes a player to do everything he can not to lose. Players that learn from their mistakes can use that knowledge to improve. Players earn the right to be confident if they are prepared. This confidence is different from being cocky. Confidence is built on preparation and knowledge, not attitude.

WHAT TO KNOW BEFORE TRYING OUT

Coaches looking for new players during a tryout want to see skills on the field. Hitters should have a strong swing and be physically able to send the ball to the outfield. A good swing using correct mechanics stands out to people assessing a player's strengths.

Throwing the ball well is another necessary skill at tryouts. A player must have the proper mechanics of throwing and be able to throw hard enough to get the ball from the outfield to the necessary base. Building enough arm strength to throw at high speeds takes time. Players should carefully increase the distance they throw at regular intervals. It is critical to build up arm strength before tryouts.

Speed is important at every level of baseball. Bases in high school are ninety feet (27 m) apart, and players should be able to run to first base in slightly more than four seconds. A slower player can work to improve his speed. This may include sprint work and strength and conditioning workouts for the lower body. Developing explosiveness in the lower body will help too.

WHAT ARE TRYOUTS LIKE?

At tryouts, players are evaluated on their speed, hitting power, arm strength, and fielding work. After warming up and stretching, the skills evaluation begins. Younger players should be able to catch consistently, while older players are evaluated on their footwork and mechanics at their positions. Expect the coaches to look for good body language, good attitude, maturity, and manners. Most coaches time the players' speed, watch their throws from right field to third and from center field to home, and watch how players hit. Catching, hitting, and throwing ability are key aspects at a tryout, and coaches look for accuracy and arm strength when players throw.

Players should show up on time in a cap, socks, cleats, baseball pants, belt, and shirt. Bring all the necessary equipment, including glove, batting gloves, and bats. Balls should be provided, but if a player wants to warm up before things are ready, he should bring his own ball too. Catchers should bring their gear. Players should be aware that they are being evaluated in everything they do during tryouts, and a mature attitude shows. Perform warm-ups to the best of your ability and show hustle. Watch the pitcher and visualize the timing for hits. Remain focused during every aspect of the tryouts.

> **"You want a guy with a good first step toward the ball."[15]**
>
> *– Major League Baseball area scout*

Catchers must be quick and have a strong arm while knowing what is happening at all times on the field. A first baseman must be quick in order to cover ground back to the base and make good catches. First basemen must also have great glove skills and flexibility to field wild throws. Second basemen need quick hands and feet. Their size isn't important as long they can make contact with the ball when batting. Third basemen need strong arms. Shortstops should be quick and agile and often are the most athletic players on the field. Left fielders need to charge the ball and have good arms.

Center fielders need to be great fielders, move very fast, and have a strong arm. Right fielders must be able to make the long throw from deep right field to third base.

The essential fielding skills for tryouts include physical skills, such as good footwork, and mental skills, such as confidence. By the time players reach high school, they should be able to play one position well, but versatility helps. Players can't be afraid of the runner and have to be able to remain in place to make the plays and get the outs. This is particularly important in double plays. A major league scout states the importance of good reactions in fielding: "You want a guy with a good first step toward the ball."[15]

Pitchers have their own set of skills needed to make the team. Each team needs several pitchers, and a pitcher should not only have a good arm but also be able to throw different pitches and place the throw wherever he needs it.

WHAT KIND OF ATTITUDE DO COACHES LOOK FOR?

A winning attitude helps a player to make a team and is noticeable from when a player first walks on the field. Coaches look for hustle and a willingness to work as they evaluate players' skills. A player who is willing to listen and is coachable has a head start over a talented player who doesn't take instruction well.

Tryouts and making the team are simply the start to playing baseball. This is just the beginning of improving in the sport. The preparation involved takes on more aspects of the player's life as he moves to the next level.

CHAPTER TWO

HOW DOES A PLAYER GET FIT
FOR BASEBALL?

Playing baseball at a high level requires talent, a drive to win, and confidence. But it takes much more to become competitive. Athleticism includes both physical skills and the proper mindset. Speed, power, flexibility, and agility are needed, but they have to be able to benefit the player's game on the field. These abilities need to be functional.

SIZE

Athletic ability is necessary to be a good baseball player, but there are no requirements for height or weight. Anyone can make it to the pros if they have the necessary skills, no matter their size. As Boston Red Sox second baseman Dustin Pedroia says, "Being big has nothing to do with playing baseball."[16] The average MLB player weighs approximately 207 pounds (94 kg), and the average height is 6 feet 2 inches (1.9 m). However, Houston Astros second baseman José Altuve is 5 feet 6 six inches (1.7 m) tall and retired pitcher Randy Johnson is 6 feet 10 inches (2.1 m) tall. Infielder Ronald Torreyes weighs about 151 pounds (68 kg), while Bartolo Colón, who pitched for the Texas Rangers in 2018, is 285 pounds (129 kg). Baseball players come in nearly every size. While larger players may be

Dustin Pedroia is shorter than the average MLB player, but his skills make him a great competitor. He won the AL Rookie of the Year Award in 2007 and was the AL MVP in 2008.

stronger, smaller players have skill sets that allow them to compete at high levels. As Altuve says, "In baseball, it doesn't matter if you're tall, skinny, fat, whatever. If you really have talent and you really love to play, I feel like you can make it."[17] Athleticism and the ability to play the game is what counts. Each position requires specific skills. Skill and drive to succeed are more important than size.

IMPROVING THROUGH PRACTICE

Practice is a critical part of playing baseball at a high level. Professional players participate in 162 games over the season, spending far more time playing games than actually practicing. They dedicate themselves to becoming better. San Francisco Giants third baseman Evan Longoria says, "I definitely think with a lot of hard work, I can be a better player than I was last year, and hopefully, continue to raise the bar every year."[18] However, high school and college baseball involves far more practice and fewer games. This makes practice very important. This is where players spend their time during the season trying to improve. At any amateur level, players need to spend this time learning, working hard, and improving.

Players have a responsibility to pay attention and work hard during practice. Coaches set the skill level of the practice. As players move up from Little League to high school and travel teams, the practices become more serious. High school requires players be at a higher level of performance, and that requires dedication.

Players at practice should have the same attitude they carry with them to game day. Begin with a defined objective for each practice. Remain in emotional control and have a plan for each pitch when batting. Focus on the process to improve and move on from mistakes. Practices can be hard, and it is a commitment for the player to attend and work hard at all of them. Altuve says, "I love playing baseball, and I always promised myself, if I had the chance, that I would work as hard as I could to be the best player I could possibly be."[19] Reviewing and evaluating after each practice helps players identify areas for improvement. These things keep players engaged and focused, making practice efficient and helpful.

PRACTICE ACTIVITIES

Practices usually begin with warm-ups, jogging, stretching, and playing catch. Catching is performed by every player in every practice. Warm-up routines and stretching allow a player to be ready to throw and bat. Warm-ups allow the muscles to perform the skills related to baseball motions while reducing the chance of injury. They also increase strength and flexibility.

Throwing with good fundamentals and form will help players throw more accurately and with more velocity. Every throw starts with the feet. Feet should be squared toward the target. Opening or closing the stance will lead to errant throws. Players should shift their weight to the back foot and then bring the weight forward by pushing with the back foot into the ground. This is what generates much of the throw's force. Throwing at game speed during practice will prepare players for the real thing.

> "I love playing baseball, and I always promised myself, if I had the chance, that I would work as hard as I could to be the best player I could possibly be."[19]
>
> – *José Altuve, Houston Astros second baseman*

Batting practices allow players to work on their swing and see pitches. Seeing the pitch, identifying it, and recognizing its location will improve anyone's batting skills. Red Sox second baseman Dustin Pedroia favors a simple approach: "I just try to see the ball and hit it."[20] Good batters focus on their batting strengths while working to address weaknesses. To improve place hitting, players can practice hitting to a specific part of the field multiple times. Repeating an action in practice helps a player perform the action in games. Knowing what

Batting cages give players a chance to swing the bat many times in quick succession. They can identify bad habits and correct them before swinging in a real game.

pitch is likely to come next can give a player an edge in reading the next pitch. Approaching each practice like it's a game will help players be ready in real games.

Practices also include infield and outfield drills. These drills involve players making decisions and relying on throwing skills to make the necessary plays at every position. In a drill called pepper, a batter lightly hits balls to fielders standing a short distance away. The fielders field the balls and then toss them back to the batter to be hit again. The drill teaches hand-eye coordination and improves a player's reaction time. Catching fly balls is another fielding skill needed because it helps players learn to track the ball in the air. Fielding is a major aspect of defense, and players should pay special attention to the fielding requirements for their

position. The Gold Glove Award is given to the best fielder at each position in the National League and American League.

WHAT KIND OF DIET HELPS BASEBALL?

An athlete's level of play is partly determined by what they do off the field. Baseball players must pay attention to their diets to stay in great physical shape. What players eat before or after games affects their play and field performance. Players should pay attention to their diet even in the off-season. Oakland Athletics first baseman and outfielder Mark Canha looks for good nutrition in his pregame meals. "Carbs, protein, goes down easy. Having digestive problems when trying to hit a 90-mph (45 km/h) fastball is no good."[21] Food is fuel for the body, and it will supply the body with energy and material to grow. All the sprints and lunges that a player does won't help him much if his body isn't supplied with good nutrition.

Eating a balanced diet is important. It should have lean proteins such as fish and grilled chicken. It should also feature fresh vegetables, fresh fruit, and complex carbohydrates such as whole grain breads and pastas. Angels first baseman and designated hitter Albert Pujols says, "I like to eat Wheaties Fuel for breakfast with fresh fruit and egg whites. For lunch, I like to eat my wife's homerun chicken, which is chicken, rice, and vegetables, and for dinner I eat grilled steak or a couple of chicken breasts with rice and vegetables."[22]

Steaming vegetables or eating them raw supplies the highest amounts of nutrients. Shellfish, turkey, and legumes also provide healthy proteins. Examples of legumes are chickpeas, lentils, peanuts, black beans, kidney beans, and soybeans. They contain high amounts of protein, carbohydrates, and fiber. Legumes are good sources of protein for players on vegetarian diets.

WHY ARE THESE FOODS NECESSARY?

Proteins are necessary to build and repair muscle. Twenty different kinds of amino acids combine to create proteins needed by the body. However, nine of the twenty amino acids are considered essential, meaning they can't be produced by the body in the amounts needed. Athletes need to get them in food. The remaining eleven amino acids are formed in the body. If athletes do not consume enough calories from carbohydrates or fats, their bodies will use amino acids for energy in place of building muscle.

Complete proteins contain all of the nine essential amino acids. Foods in this category include chicken, beef, and fish. Incomplete proteins do not contain all of the nine essential amino acids and are mostly found in plants and grains. Eating grains and nuts that are incomplete proteins, along with other incomplete proteins such as dried beans, peas, or peanuts or peanut butter, can create complete proteins. Having a peanut butter sandwich on wheat bread, beans with cornbread, or rice and beans provides complete proteins that can help fuel and build an athlete's body.

Athletes need more than the average amount of protein, depending on their activity level, intensity level, and activity length. Proteins should be eaten several hours before the practice or game.

A healthful mix of grains, vegetables, and protein provides athletes with the nutrients they need to play their best. Cutting out junk food that is high in fat and sugar can also improve an athlete's game.

Eating protein shortly after exercise, too, provides the best results for developing and repairing muscles.

Center fielder Billy Burns eats a small portion of pasta with chicken or steak or a turkey sandwich on wheat for a good mix of protein and complex carbohydrates before a game. Pregame meals should be small, healthy, and a source of complex carbohydrates. Burns tries not to eat too much before a game, saying he just wants "something to fill my stomach to get out there, not to fill me up too much."[23]

Former New York Yankees first baseman Mark Teixeira started his day off with a healthy breakfast of turkey bacon and a smoothie of coconut yogurt, spinach, and frozen berries. Sandwiches play a big part in pregame meals. Cincinnati Reds pitcher Matt Wisler enjoys a bacon, lettuce, and tomato sandwich, while former Atlanta Braves right fielder Jeff Francoeur chose peanut butter and jelly.

Baseball players perform various short-duration actions that need high power. Batting and pitching wind-ups need a burst of energy in a short amount of time. Players train for strength and power in practices and workouts. Building muscle with protein helps the body prepare for these exertions.

CARBOHYDRATES AND FATS

Carbohydrates are turned into glycogen, providing short, strong bursts of energy in the muscles. Different energy needs occur during baseball, which has high energy-expending periods and times of rest. After getting a hit, a player sprints to first base using energy provided by the carbs that were eaten earlier. Choosing food that supplies steady, even levels of blood sugar pregame is better than a food that gives players a fast but short-term amount of energy. Carbohydrates differ in how they provide energy. Carbohydrates are important for quality athletic performance and prevent the body from using only fats for energy.

Fats provide the most energy of the three main nutrient groups. Carbs and proteins contain four calories for every gram, but fats have nine calories per gram. They are the main energy provider for a resting body. Fats provide long-term energy too. Fats carry out other vital actions in the athlete's body. In the correct amounts, fats are

SURGERIES

In recent years there has been a rise in the number of Tommy John surgeries. The surgery repairs a torn ulnar collateral ligament in the elbow. A tendon from somewhere else in the body is used to replace the torn ligament. This stabilizes the elbow and restores the range of motion in the arm. The first time this surgery was used was on pitcher Tommy John in 1974.

Many doctors urge a conservative approach to frayed ligaments and sore elbows. Rest and rehabilitation is often prescribed if the player likely won't play at the next level. The surgery isn't foolproof and can have complications, even if the procedure goes well. Many professional pitchers have undergone the procedure with great success, and so the number of youth players requesting the surgery continues to grow.

Because pitching requires an unnatural motion, it also requires plenty of rest, especially in youth baseball. Ligaments in the elbow fray and require a period of rest to heal. When pitchers join off-season teams, their ligaments may not get enough time to recover.

necessary. Baseball players can perform their best when fueled by a diet that supplies all of these nutrients.

Players should aim to eat plenty of healthy foods, but they should also avoid some kinds of unhealthy foods. Avoid processed foods lacking nutrients or containing too much sugar. Greasy, fatty, processed foods have no place in a well-balanced diet. Fast foods are especially high in fat and calories. These foods can be an occasional treat, but they are not part of a healthy diet. Angels center fielder Mike Trout says, "As I get older every year, I'm eating better. As a kid, who can turn down chips and candy? But I'm getting better."[24]

Besides protein, carbohydrates, and fats, there are other substances the body needs to get from food. Eating five servings of

Staying hydrated during games is not just a way to play better but also a safety issue. Baseball is played in hot summer months, when it can be easy to become dehydrated outdoors.

fruits and vegetables provides additional nutrients such as vitamins and minerals. Different vitamins and minerals are found in different foods. These substances are important to different functions in the body.

Vitamin B2 helps the body break down and digest food. Vitamin C helps the body fight off disease and supports healthy eye function. Some vitamins are made by the body, but a healthy and balanced diet will provide the rest of the vitamins that athletes need to play their best.

HYDRATION

Players need to stay hydrated by drinking water and sports drinks. During practices and hot summer games, players will sweat. The body loses water

> **"As I get older every year, I'm eating better. As a kid, who can turn down chips and candy? But I'm getting better."**[24]
>
> *— Mike Trout, Los Angeles Angels center fielder*

and electrolytes, substances critical to many bodily functions. Players can lose over one pound (0.45 kg) of water through sweat by the time they realize they are thirsty. To stay well hydrated, players should drink 16 ounces (0.47 L) of water an hour before the game and an additional 6 ounces (0.18 L) every other inning. It is even more important to stay hydrated during humid summer games and double headers.

Some players prefer sports drinks over drinking water, but sports drinks often have a lot of sugar and artificial sweeteners. In most cases, water is the best option to hydrate an athlete. However, hot days, double headers, or playing on back-to-back days can make a player more likely to cramp, and sports drinks excel at replenishing the electrolytes to keep a player going in these conditions.

CHAPTER THREE

WHAT TAKES PLACE ON
GAME DAY?

Game day is an important day for players at any level. Youth league and high school players may have other activities scheduled. Baseball might be a big part of a player's life, but it is not the only part. Minor leaguers and professionals have a bit more control over their schedules on games days, but everything players do before the game can affect their performance. Players should keep their focus on the game once it starts. Being distracted can lead to mental errors in the batter's box and in the field. Angels outfielder Mike Trout described his own feelings about game day: "The first game of your career is obviously the biggest, but you still get the jitters, you still get the adrenaline rush before every game. A lot of people don't realize that, but it's true."[25] A player's attitude, mental state, mindset, and ability to visualize are key to playing their best.

Attitude includes the thoughts, actions, and reactions of a player. A positive attitude is the start to a successful game day. A positive attitude comes from a good mental state. Talent is valuable for successful teams, but a positive attitude is a sign of a winning team. Teams that consistently win have a good attitude stemming from the coach down to the individual players. They are confident without

Playing in a real game, regardless of the level of competition, brings a new level of pressure that is not present in practice. Mental focus is critical for a player to perform his best in a game situation.

being cocky. Winning attitudes are part of a player's way of life, and that includes baseball.

Mental toughness plays a big part in a player's focus and attitude about baseball. A mentally tough player remains calm and believes in himself and that he can perform well. Philadelphia Phillies outfielder

Andrew McCutchen says, "In order to be better, you should expect to be better."[26] Mental toughness can be developed with positive thinking and self-confidence. Confidence comes from adequate preparation and knowing that you have done everything possible to get ready.

The best mindset includes sticking with the game in every success and failure. Failure leads to learning. Players who are of good character, react well under stress, keep their minds open to learning, and are coachable have the most success. Coaches aim to instill a winning attitude, but players must take the responsibility for it. Players need to know that even if they play their best, they may fail. Physical errors happen but mental errors can be overcome. A good player remains positive following failure and uses that to learn and motivate him in the future.

Visualization is a critical component of being successful as a baseball player. A player should picture what they will do before doing it, whether it involves batting, fielding, or throwing. After a time, visualization becomes easier. Positive visualization creates positive emotions inside a player. This develops into strong play. Players can identify the positive emotions and focus on them. Develop a plan for visualizing what needs to be done and relax physically and mentally. Visualization works, but it is a skill that must be developed.

WHAT MAKES A GOOD TEAM PLAYER?

Baseball is a team sport. Individuals work to perform at their highest level, but being a team player is crucial. Teamwork begins with a team defining its overall purpose, setting goals, and creating plans to achieve those goals. Just as with individuals, setting clear goals and planning strategies to achieve them makes the team much more likely to achieve those goals. It also makes certain all the team members understand their roles on the team.

Players accept their roles and do what they can to help the team, even if it requires sacrificing their desired position or batting according to what the coach needs to help the team. Competition grows at each level of play. Good teammates help each other out when needed, and teams work together to find a way to win. As Cincinnati Reds right fielder Yasiel Puig says,

> **"As long as the team is pulling together, I'm happy to be a part of it."**[27]
>
> – *Yasiel Puig, Cincinnati Reds right fielder*

"As long as the team is pulling together, I'm happy to be a part of it."[27] Winning takes a particular mindset, and a team must develop that attitude. Additionally, team players focus on what they can control and disregard what they cannot control. Being part of a team takes a commitment beyond the individual players. These values begin developing from a young age. New York Yankees outfielder Aaron Judge says his father emphasized the importance of sacrifice and teamwork, and he took those lessons to heart.

Members of the team then work to perform their jobs from the team's plans. Players adjust according to advice and feedback from teammates and coaches. Teams evaluate their actions and adjust to make sure they are headed toward success. Philadelphia Phillies outfielder Bryce Harper says, "I want my teammates to know I have their backs."[28]

Coming together with teammates and trusting coaches can help unify a team and increase its chances of success. It's important to not be a selfish player.

Coaches prefer baseball players who listen, are open, take helpful suggestions, and want to improve. This is called being coachable. They also want athletes who are team players and work well with their teammates. Individual statistics and goals must be put aside to be a good team player. As Texas Rangers infielder Asdrubal Cabrera says, "I'm going to do my best to help the team play hard and help the team win. . . . I'm just coming to play baseball."[29]

Besides relying on teammates, players look to the coaching staff. Players trust their coaches and the knowledge they bring to practices and the games. Coaches need their players to show up, work hard, and be coachable. Players count on their teammates to work and make their team goals achievable. Teams need every individual to perform at his best every game.

> **"It was amazing just to know I contributed at some point. These guys picked up all the slack that I left. That's what a team does."**[30]
>
> *– Mookie Betts, Boston Red Sox left fielder*

Performing well is important, but it must be done for the overall good of the team and not for the players alone. After a shaky performance in a game his team still won, Red Sox left fielder Mookie Betts says, "It was amazing just to know I contributed at some point. These guys picked up all the slack that I left. That's what a team does."[30]

THE PSYCHOLOGY BEHIND THE TEAMWORK

Baseball differs from other sports because it involves a one-on-one showdown in the midst of a larger team competition. The batter and pitcher face off against each other, and the other players on the field must react to what they do. In most other team sports, all the players continuously work together. But in baseball, all the attention in the stadium is on the pitcher and batter during an at-bat. Baseball players must prepare not only physically but also mentally to endure this pressure. A focus on mental preparation has become much more prominent in recent years in MLB.

In order to react to all of the situations that arise in a game, players have to mentally prepare and be ready. Detroit Tigers third baseman

Jeimer Candelario says, "You have to control your emotions and control yourself. You just breathe and calm down."[31] Players must concentrate on a way that works for them to relieve tension and allows them to focus. Many players find a fixed point to look at in order to focus and relax. Staying with a regular routine allows players to concentrate on their job and perform at their best.

Chicago White Sox pitcher Carson Fulmer doesn't look at a single item. He prefers to look at the crowd in general, which becomes a blurry image. "That lets me clear my mind and focus on the glove, and I'm ready to go and let my body take over. It gives me an extra second to just breathe and center myself."[32]

Players need to be aware of where their focus is and accept when a problem occurs. Then they must move on. Good players focus on what is next during the game and prepare for that. Having a routine helps players get ready for a game both physically and mentally. It helps during high-stress situations, such as their first major league game or during the playoffs.

GETTING GAME READY

Players arrive early to prepare for the game, often arriving at 2:00 p.m. for a 7:00 p.m. game. They can eat a light snack and then change into their practice workout uniform. Many players go to the field for some stretching or drills. The team stretches together at a time assigned by the manager. This is often around 3:30 in the minor leagues and closer to 4:00 in the major leagues. Batting practice follows, and the team leaves for the clubhouse so the visiting team can have the field. Some players take a nap or visualize game situations to prepare for the game.

Stretching is an important game-day routine for players. They prepare their bodies for the movements they'll be making during the game.

Players eat a pregame meal, usually including fruits, vegetables, sandwiches, or other snacks. Players don't eat anything heavy. Sometimes players order their own food if they want something special. After the meal is a time to relax and let food settle. Many players watch television or play games. Sometimes pitchers, catchers, and the pitching coach meet to talk about the other team's strengths and weaknesses. By 6:15, players dress for the game. The starting pitcher begins a routine of stretching and throwing with the catcher. The opponent's pitcher is discussed before the rest of the players take the field. Albert Pujols says, "Preparation is very important. The pitcher is going to do his job and prepare for you so you as a hitter must do the same. I always watch videotape of pitchers before the game and even sometimes during."[33]

SUPERSTITIONS IN BASEBALL

Superstitions abound in baseball. Some are well-known practices that are part of players' game day routines. Aaron Judge is known as a slugger, but his superstition with Dubble Bubble bubblegum revolves around defense. Just before the first pitch, he chews two pieces. He does not spit out the gum until he makes an out.

Astros outfielder George Springer includes a superstition that began in college. If he has been hitting well, he wears the same socks. He does wash them, though. However, if his hitting goes badly, he switches them. Pitcher Matt Garza eats Popeye's chicken each time he starts. Chicago Cubs teammates Anthony Rizzo and Ben Zobrist, and their former teammate Dexter Fowler, admitted their superstitions on late night television. Zobrist and Fowler sat on the same spot on the bench every time. Rizzo stated that after breaking his phone during the 2016 National League Championship Series, he wouldn't get it repaired until the playoffs ended. However, José Altuve says he has no pregame superstitions or rituals.

A set routine allows players to relax and remove some of the distractions that occur pregame, allowing the body and mind to relax and keep their focus on the game. A player's routine can be as simple as following the team routine, including riding the bus to the game together, performing the warm-ups, and being in the locker room together. Team routines help players so they are ready for the pregame preparation.

Human bodies react to repetition, and it puts players in the mindset for a game. As soon as players arrive at the ballpark, they begin their pregame routine. Baseball drills are designed to loosen up the muscles and get the player into a mental state where he can focus. Additionally, being warmed up and loose helps prevent injuries, so warm-ups need to be done with a serious attitude and should not

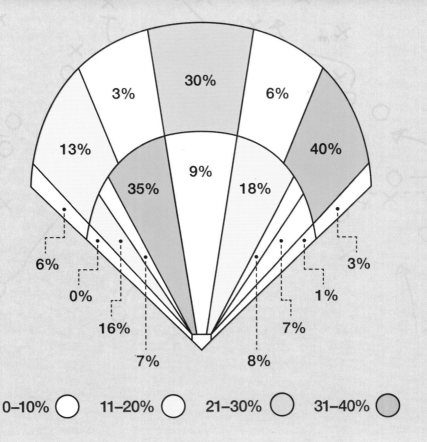

0–10% ○ 11–20% ○ 21–30% ○ 31–40% ○

A spray chart is a useful tool to visually show tendencies or percentages. For baseball they are used to show how often a batter hits to each part of the field. This chart is for a right-handed hitter who hits the ball all over the field. It shows where outfield hits land and where infield hits land. The outfield percentages add up to approximately 100 percent, as do the infield percentages (they do not add to exactly 100 due to rounding). Teams break down and analyze opposing batters and pitchers with graphs and statistics. This is an actual scouting report for second baseman Nick Madrigal. Fielders can learn batters' tendencies and then plan where to position themselves for each player.

Pregame batting practice is a key part of players' routines. Players can fine-tune their hitting one more time before the game.

be skipped. Players have time to stretch, run, play catch, and focus on the game before taking the field. Each player establishes a routine that works for him. Every routine may differ, but the value of simply having a routine develops a better player. Many players even become superstitious with their routines.

Some warm-up drills include infield and outfield, but in MLB, batting practice is usually the focus. It is generally determined by the coaches and done in rounds. The first round lets players get the feel of the ball and set their timing. The second round involves situational hitting for that game. The remaining rounds include place hitting. Once batting practice is completed, players' routines vary.

IN THE GAME

Routines continue throughout the game. When players move to the on-deck circle, they may stretch, swing to loosen up, or swing with a donut on their bat. This is a weight that helps players increase their swing speed. Good players watch the pitcher and visualize hitting. They consciously relax and steady their breathing. Once they go to the batter's box, they are ready for the first pitch. In the batter's box, most players follow a routine.

Postgame, players shower, change, and eat a meal. What they have depends on the clubhouse manager, but it incorporates the nutrients players need after a game. Some players stay and work out. Then they head home. Establishing a routine not only helps players focus on their job but allows them the ability to remain consistent in their life, even if they are not playing well or are on the road. A strong physical and mental routine helps them consistently be the best they can be.

CHAPTER FOUR

WHAT DOES IT TAKE TO MOVE TO
THE NEXT LEVEL?

It's not easy to move to the next level in baseball, and the statistics show this. The percentage of baseball players moving from high school to the National Collegiate Athletic Association (NCAA) level is 7.1 percent, with only 2.1 percent playing in a Division I (DI) program, 2.2 percent going to a Division II (DII) program, and 2.8 percent going to a Division III (DIII) program.

The percentage of players making a professional team after having played in the NCAA is 9.5 percent. Of the 1,215 draft picks in 2017, MLB teams selected 735 players from a pool of 7,773 eligible NCAA players. The chances of high school players being drafted is only 0.5 percent. Once a player is drafted, they do not instantly play in the major leagues. Players drafted by MLB teams begin in the minor leagues. There are more than 200 minor league teams but only thirty major league teams.

FOCUSING ON BASEBALL VERSUS PLAYING MULTIPLE SPORTS

Most baseball players at some point think about playing a different sport that they also like during baseball's off-season. Or players might think about playing baseball exclusively. Some people argue that

Minor league play is a key step on the road to MLB. Players who excel in the minor leagues can move up to the next level.

specializing early makes a better player in baseball, believing that football or basketball skills don't translate to the baseball field.

Athleticism frequently allows baseball players to excel in multiple sports. However, a player who concentrates solely on baseball tends to be a higher quality player at the higher levels. Some high-level athletes may play two or more sports, but this is an unusual route to stepping up to the next level. Kyler Murray, an Oakland Athletics draft pick, also won the Heisman Trophy as a quarterback at the University of Oklahoma. He entered the 2019 National Football League (NFL) draft. He said, "Moving forward, I am firmly and fully committing my life and time to becoming an NFL quarterback."[34]

However, playing only a single sport is not for everyone. Training requires a commitment and isn't something worked on during one season out of the year. To be competitive, training has to be at the core of a player's time year round. Otherwise, most players will fall behind. Outfielder Curtis Granderson said, "Basketball was always my sport. It just took me until my second year of college for me to realize that I was a better baseball player than a basketball player. But basketball was always my number one love. Finally found out I was better at baseball and chose to pursue that route."[35]

HOW CAN PLAYERS MOVE UP?

Moving to the next level in baseball takes a combination of talent, inner drive, and focus. As the competition increases, players have to be willing to push themselves to improve and stay willing to learn. At every level, this means working harder and working more. Improving takes time and effort, and moving to the next level requires a lot of improving. Good players are not satisfied with where they are. Instead, they work to get as far as possible. This could mean making the varsity squad, earning a college offer, making the next minor league level, or even going from starting on an MLB team to being named to the All-Star team. Players should never become complacent with where they are in their game or on their team. Ed Servais, a college coach at Creighton University, says, "It seems like sometimes when you have a lot of guys back that played a lot the year before, everyone assumes they're going to be better. . . . That's a bad way of looking at things."[36]

As a player moves upward, he is used to being one of the best and the center of attention. Players may be surprised to find that they are now closer to average or even the bottom when they jump to a new level of competition. They need to realize that this is typical when someone moves to a more elite level of play. Hard work is needed to keep up. The hours spent working on baseball will fill more of their time. They are constantly faced with new failures which can wear down a player. It's a mental adjustment as well as a physical one. Maintaining the right mindset allows a player to improve and continue to move up. Excellent players realize every baseball player experiences failures and that good players learn from their failures. Players have to play for their team and not get caught up in their personal statistics.

> **"It seems like sometimes when you have a lot of guys back that played a lot the year before, everyone assumes they're going to be better. . . . That's a bad way of looking at things."**[36]
>
> – Ed Servais, Creighton University head coach

THE DIFFERENT LEVELS

Baseball exists at different levels as a player's skills develop. Players move from community recreation leagues toward junior varsity, then toward varsity in high school, travel teams, collegiate baseball, junior college (JUCO) teams, summer league teams, area code baseball, minor league teams, and professional baseball teams. Because the competition grows at each level, fewer players move up. Those who do advance usually display traits common among excellent players.

High school players try out for the varsity team. Some freshmen will be assigned to the freshman team, but excellent freshmen can still make the varsity roster. If they fall short, they can try out again the

Making the varsity baseball team can be exciting. However, high school players must be sure to balance their studies with their athletic goals.

following year. Know the game and practice consistently to keep the skills fresh. Repetition is key in high school.

Working during the off-season is another way to prepare for varsity baseball. Attending baseball camps and training sessions during the off-season months will give players a high level of instruction. Players should use the off-season for weight training and conditioning to maintain muscles and reduce the possibility of injury during the season.

Proper nutrition is vital for a high-quality athlete, and following proper nutritional guidelines is key to keeping fit for school baseball. Maintain a positive attitude even if mistakes occur and make a good impression on the coach. Many factors besides talent work to feed success in varsity baseball.

MOVING UP THROUGH TRAVELING TEAMS

Moving up to the next level of baseball sometimes can be done through baseball travel teams. Youth travel baseball provides weekend tournaments for organizations such as United States Specialty Sports Association (USSSA) Baseball. Teams may travel for tournaments from state to state, although a lot of teams play locally. There are often four games in a weekend. Teams are formed by coaches, and players must pay fees and buy their uniforms once they make the team.

Travel teams are not without some controversy, however. They may be costly and involve driving long distances for practices. There may be a lack of playing time if a less skilled player makes the team but doesn't play regularly. Players will spend a large amount of time with the team, so it's important to have good teammates. Each player needs to decide if a travel team is better for their development compared with local baseball leagues.

When choosing a travel team, families need to consider the coach, the person most involved with player improvement. Coaches have the most impact on players, and a good coach will be concerned with developing skills as well as the player as a person. Good coaches run organized, smooth practices that have little downtime. The coaches focus on mechanics and correct problems.

When a player is considering trying out for a travel team, it may be best to wait until age fourteen because this is when 75 percent of youth playing sports quit. Other aspects of life begin to change, and some players choose to cut baseball to make room for other interests. Paying to join the team, travel, and purchasing uniforms and gear may not be worth the investment if it is not something the player will continue to pursue. Local recreational teams can provide training and skills, and players can then move to travel teams if they

When young players join traveling teams, their parents often make significant investments in their children's sports. For example, parents may buy special gear that allows players to practice batting at home.

choose to keep playing. Playing baseball requires skill, desire, and aptitude, so playing for travel teams does not guarantee success, nor does it ensure a player will make the high school team. Travel ball can provide additional training, so players must consider what is in their best interest.

JUNIOR COLLEGE BASEBALL

JUCO offers another way to continue playing baseball at a higher level. JUCO baseball is serious and competitive. Taking this route can be a step to playing at the professional level. JUCO baseball provides playing time and opportunities to be scouted while providing either a way into a Division I program or a chance to enter the MLB Draft without playing the required three years at the college level. Attending a JUCO is also cheaper than four-year college. There are no draft eligibility regulations that require JUCO players to stay in school. They can be drafted after their first year, and they are even able to be re-drafted after their second year. Approximately 326 JUCO players are drafted every year. That means approximately 10 percent of drafted players come from JUCO. Bryce Harper was the number one pick in the 2010 MLB Draft following his stint at the College of Southern Nevada. Brandon Belt and Albert Pujols are other professional players who began in JUCO.

JUCO also offers the opportunity to move to a DI school. Belt moved from San Jacinto Community College and then transferred to the University of Texas. He was selected in the fifth round of the 2009 MLB Draft by the San Francisco Giants.

PLAYING AT THE COLLEGE LEVEL

The step up from high school baseball or travel teams to Division I, II, or III requires a large amount of talent and significant statistics from earlier baseball experience to make the team. College senior Garrett Snyder credits his coaches at Ithaca College for his development: "I'm a completely different player. I can't thank the coaches enough for helping me out. I look back at my high school recruiting video, and I don't know why they even considered me to play here. I was not even close to where I am now. We have great coaches who have a ton of experience. . . . We're really grateful to have them."[37]

College baseball involves more difficult strength and conditioning programs that require a higher level of physical fitness and endurance. The increase in training from high school to college is significant.

College baseball draws more interest and bigger crowds than high school baseball. It is one more step on the way to the major leagues.

Players must adjust to the speed and change in physical demands of college baseball and reach and maintain a high level of execution. Prepare for college with summer workouts. Check with the coach to determine what is required of players and faithfully complete the off-season training. This helps develop a good workout habit. During the school year, strength and conditioning are often done on the players' own time. Regular workouts contribute to a successful college baseball experience.

University or college competition in baseball offers a chance to learn, compete, and achieve a higher level of success. Student-athletes have access to excellent coaching, facilities, trainers, and equipment, along with academic help and medical support. College baseball levels vary by the schools themselves. Baseball players can target a Division I, Division II, or Division III school. Besides meeting the academic requirements for entering college, players aiming for a DI or DII school must register with the NCAA Eligibility Center. Players wishing to attend and play baseball for a DIII school do not need to register.

Top level players are recruited for colleges and universities. Players interested in a particular program can apply to that school and let the baseball coach know of their interest. They can send videos of their play, but more often camps and tournaments from the summer before their junior year of high school are used for recruiting players. These camps need to be ones the targeted school coaches follow, however. Players can create an athletic profile and attend showcases. It's also important to be eligible academically. They can take college entrance exams and know what each university expects of its incoming students.

WALKING ON

Walking on is another way to try out and make the college baseball team. NCAA DII and III, along with JUCOs, often hold tryouts to give walk-on players an opportunity to make the team. A few DI colleges offer tryouts for walk-on players, but often they have already filled their rosters and have no room. If a player's coach knows or played with a college coach, sometimes the player's coach can get the player a tryout.

DI schools are usually larger, have a greater athletic budget, contain a wider variety of academic choices, and give out more athletic scholarships than DII schools. DII and DIII programs offer less financial and structural support, but they still provide a high level of education for players.

THE DRAFT AND AREA CODE BASEBALL

Area Code Baseball is one of the best ways for teenage players to get noticed and potentially drafted. Players need to fill out an Area Code Player Profile, which will be sent to the nearest regional office. Chosen players are invited to an MLB regional tryout, and invitations come from the recommendations of MLB scouts. Players that make it are listed on the Area Code roster, and teams are chosen based on their performance at tryouts. Each team contains twenty-five to thirty players.

From the 3,000 invitations mailed out, only around 200 players are assigned a team. Both Area Code Baseball Games and MLB-run regional tryouts have no cost. Area code players can pay to attend Area Code Baseball Instructs, which give athletes the chance to develop skills and learn from the MLB scouts in charge of Area Code Games teams. They may also choose to pay for a video and written assessment package. Chosen Area Code players pay only for their travel to the games. Sixty-five players from the 2016 Area Code games were chosen in the 2017 MLB Draft.

At the Area Code games, eight regional teams compete over five days in August. MLB and Scouting Bureau scouts attend and evaluate players. The tournament introduces these elite players to MLB personnel and is followed by the major league draft the following June.

TRYING OUT FOR THE MAJOR LEAGUES

Players wanting to play in Major League Baseball do not usually try out. The Major League Baseball first-year player draft takes place in June. All thirty major clubs participate. To be eligible for the draft, players have to be a resident of Canada or the United States, including Puerto Rico and other US territories, and have never signed a major

The Houston Astros held tryouts in Corpus Christi, Texas, in the summer of 2014. Many major league teams offer prospective players a chance to show off their skills.

or minor league contract. If a player from another country enrolls and attends high school or college in the United States, they can also be considered. High school graduates who have not yet attended college, college players who have completed their junior or senior year, and all JUCO players are eligible for the draft.

Before 2015, the Major League Scouting Bureau used to hold a series of summer tryouts at no charge and send the information to every MLB team. This allowed overlooked players to have a chance to be seen and evaluated on the five tools. Making a team through tryouts didn't happen often, but it gave players the chance to play in front of a pro scout. However, this process was stopped in 2015, and now prospective players can be invited to try out for a minor league team. Some professional teams hold their own tryouts. The dates and locations are found each year in April or May on the MLB or team websites.

PLAYING IN THE MINORS

Baseball is currently the only sport with a large development organization. The minor league teams, or farm teams, are composed of players drafted or signed as free agents by a major league team. All thirty major league teams have a system of minor league teams that supply players as they develop.

Rookie ball or short-season ball allows drafted players to become accustomed to the higher level of baseball because the draft occurs mid-season. The travel is not as extensive, and the players have the opportunity to acclimate.

The next step is Single-A ball, which is divided into low-A ball and high-A ball. Players participate in spring training to get ready for 140 games over five months. High school draftees usually go to low-A ball, while college players tend to start at high-A ball.

Double-A ball brings players closer to the majors but weeds out players lacking talent to make it to the major leagues. Those players who do make it to this level have the potential to move up to the majors. Competition is better, and pitchers are more capable than at Single-A baseball. This level mostly has players who will be moving up.

Triple-A ball is nearest the major leagues and contains many types of players. There are potential stars, even though excellent players may skip Triple-A and move directly to the majors. Some Triple-A players have had major league experience, and others may

SABERMETRICS

Bill James developed the theory of sabermetrics in 1980, defining it as "the search for objective knowledge about baseball." Sabermetrics relies on statistics or mathematical analysis to study baseball. This analysis often goes against traditional measures of baseball success, such as batting averages and number of pitcher wins. The film *Moneyball* popularized the idea, although it had been around in some form much earlier.

In the middle of the 1800s, Henry Chadwick developed the box score and kept count of hits, home runs, and total bases, which led to the metrics records of batting average and slugging percentages. Branch Rickey had a statistician named Allan Roth evaluate players and their skills in the 1940s for the Brooklyn Dodgers. Manager Earl Weaver used a set of cards to manage information about his Baltimore Orioles players in the 1970s. This mathematical way of putting baseball statistics to use eventually changed the way players were examined.

Phil Birnbaum, "A Guide to Sabermetric Research," SABR, n.d., www.sabr.org.

be rehabbing from injuries. Some MLB players are sent down to hone their skills with the idea of returning. Texas Rangers second baseman Rougned Odor was hitting .144 in 2015. He said of his return to Triple-A ball, "I was swinging at a lot of bad pitches, I know that. I was not like me. I didn't feel like me. I wasn't hitting good. I kind of knew they might [demote me]. They sent me down and now I'm going to work. I don't want to get mad because if I do, I'll block myself from getting better."[38]

In the minors, new players enter each year. Unless some players are released, there is no room for the new team members. Many reasons exist for releasing players, but moving up is not easy and not everyone makes it to the majors. After a player is released, his information is sent out to other teams. After packing, the released player leaves and returns home, courtesy of the team. After that, they are on their own. Some released players sign up with an independent ball team, but others find employment outside of baseball. There are some who do make it to the big leagues, but it is not likely. Baseball is a difficult career, and it's hard to become a major league player.

INDEPENDENT LEAGUE BALL

Not every baseball player can sign with a major league team. Independent leagues give players a place to showcase their talent or continue playing baseball. In 2019, there were six main independent leagues. They are the American Association, the Atlantic League, the Can-Am League (Canada and Northeast), the Frontier League, the Pecos League, and the Pacific Association League. The Pecos and Pacific Leagues are for young players and don't have players moving up to the major leagues. The odds are low for Independent League players to be selected by minor league teams, and very few make it to the majors. Pitchers are at an advantage. They are 40 percent more likely to be chosen for the majors compared with position players.

> **"When you're a first-round pick and you get to the big leagues at twenty-two, there's almost a sense that you've got to mature."**[39]
>
> – Evan Longoria, San Francisco Giants third baseman

MAJOR LEAGUES

A drafted player has to sign with the baseball club by August 15. If he chooses to enter a four-year college full time, he no longer is affiliated with that team. Players who were drafted but that do not sign can be drafted in another year. Eligible players who are not selected become free

In the 2000s, Major League Baseball Advanced Media began installing pitch tracking hardware in some MLB stadiums. A system called Statcast has built on this work, using advanced technology that can collect baseball data so it can be analyzed. By 2015, Statcast was placed in all 30 MLB stadiums. It consists of two kinds of tracking systems. One is a Trackman Doppler Radar device installed behind home plate. It follows the motion of the baseball, showing pitch speed, spin rate, pitch movement, arm strength, and many other aspects. The second part is an HD ChyronHego camera. This camera contains six stereoscopic cameras in groups along the foul line. It tracks player motion on the field and provides a way to follow speed, distance, and other parts of the players' motions.

Statcast incorporates data on offense, defense, and pitch statistics along with all the aspects of each piece of the play being broken down. Statcast is used to quantify and analyze players more objectively and show a player's possible future results. Mike Petriello of MLB.com believes that the future of Statcast is bright. He says, "It's like the bottom of the second inning really, so far as all this goes."

Quoted in R.J. Anderson, "How Statcast Has Changed MLB and Why Not Everybody Seems All That Happy About It," *CBS Sports*, June 6, 2017. www.cbssports.com.

agents and can sign with any baseball club unless the player enters or returns to a four-year college or JUCO. Reaching the goal of major league play brings on a new sense of responsibility. Giants third baseman Evan Longoria says, "When you're a first-round pick and you get to the big leagues at twenty-two, there's almost a sense that you've got to mature."[39]

Once a player reaches the major leagues, there is no guarantee he will remain there. Injuries, poor performance, and trades can cut a player's career short. However, if a player's passion is to play baseball, the satisfaction of playing well at any level brings an achievement that will never be forgotten.

SOURCE NOTES

INTRODUCTION: BECOMING THE BEST

1. Quoted in Mark Feinsand, "Trout's HS Coach Surprised by Degree of Success," *MLB.com*, June 9, 2017. www.mlb.com.

2. Quoted in Feinsand, "Trout's HS Coach Surprised by Degree of Success."

3. Quoted in Adam Kilgore, "Baseball's Dilemma: Mike Trout Is MLB's Ultimate All-Star, and Yet He Is Not a Star," *Washington Post*, July 16, 2018. www.washingtonpost.com.

4. Quoted in Alden Gonzalez, "Mike Trout's Relentless Quest to Get Even Better," *ESPN*, September 30, 2018. www.espn.com.

5. Quoted in Andrea Thompson, "Mind Games: What Makes a Great Baseball Player Great," *LiveScience*, October 26, 2007. www.livescience.com.

6. Quoted in Kristie Ackert, "Astros Hope Jose Altuve's Rare Show of Emotion Continues with More Offense in Game 7 vs. Yankees," *New York Daily News*, April 7, 2018. www.nydailynews.com.

7. Quoted in "Little Leaguer Mo'Ne David Writes a Memoir," *Washington Post*, n.d. www.washingtonpost.com.

CHAPTER ONE: WHAT DOES IT TAKE TO MAKE THE TEAM?

8. Quoted in Mike Petriello, "Mike Trout Has Improved His Defense in Center," *MLB.com*, May 30, 2018. www.mlb.com.

9. Quoted in Tyler Kepner, "Outsize Production," *New York Times*, August 19, 2014. www.nytimes.com.

10. Quoted in Larry Stone, "Mariners Remain Confident: 'Our Mindset Is Just Trying to Get to the Playoffs,'" *Seattle Times*, July 17, 2018. www.seattletimes.com.

11. Quoted in Fred Goodall, "Baseball," *Los Angeles Times*, April 5, 2009. www.latimes.com.

12. Quoted in Bob Nightingale, "Verlander on Kate Upton, Taco Bell, Hall of Fame," *USA Today*, October 22, 2012. www.usatoday.com.

13. Quoted in Dave Golokhov, "Albert Pujols Interview," *AskMen*, n.d. https://me.askmen.com.

14. Quoted in Dan Israeli, "The 5-Tool Baseball Player Workout," *Men's Journal*, June 28, 2018. www.mensjournal.com.

15. Quoted in John Perrotto, "Lone Star: Altuve Stands Tall Despite Astros' Struggles," *USA Today*, May 29, 2013. www.usatoday.com.

CHAPTER TWO: HOW DOES A PLAYER GET FIT FOR BASEBALL?

16. Quoted in Robert W. Cohen, *The 50 Greatest Players in Red Sox History*. Guilford, CT: Lyons Press Fish, 2018. p. 138.

17. Quoted in Tyler Kepner, "To Measure Altuve, Just Watch Him Soar," *New York Times*, October 24, 2017. www.nytimes.com.

18. Quoted in Goodall, "Baseball."

19. Quoted in John Perrotto, "Novelty No More: Astros' Jose Altuve in the Conversation as One of Baseball's Best," *USA Today*, July 11, 2016. www.usatoday.com.

20. Quoted in Adam Kilgore, "Swing Man," *Boston Globe*, September 12, 2008. www.boston.com.

21. Quoted in Abby Reisner, "Big League Chew," *Tasting Table*, April 14, 2016. www.tastingtable.com.

22. Quoted in Golokhov, "Albert Pujols Interview."

23. Quoted in Maria Scinto, "A Diet for Baseball Players," *Livestrong*, September 11, 2017. www.livestrong.com.

24. Quoted in Lynn Hoppes, "Offbeat Questions with Angels' Mike Trout," *ESPN*, April 10, 2013. www.espn.com.

CHAPTER THREE: WHAT TAKES PLACE ON GAME DAY?

25. Quoted in Paul Eide, "Major League MVP Mike Trout on the Secret to Succeeding in Your 20s," *AskMen*, March 31, 2016. www.askmen.com.

26. Quoted in Jerry Krasnick, "A Reason to Believe in Pittsburgh," *ESPN*, April 9, 2010. www.espn.com.

27. Quoted in "Lights, Camera, Action: Yasiel Puig Stars in L.A.," *Oakland Press*, June 10, 2013. www.theoaklandpress.com.

28. Quoted in Paul White, "Unwritten Rules Reign," *USA Today*, May 8, 2012. www.usatoday.com.

29. Quoted in James Wagner, "Meet the New Second Baseman: Asdrubal Cabrera Arrives at Nationals Park," *Washington Post*, August 1, 2014. www.washingtonpost.com.

30. Quoted in Nicole Yang, "What the Red Sox Had to Say After Winning the 2018 World Series," *Boston Globe*, October 29, 2018. www.boston.com.

31. Quoted in Jared Wyllys, "Going Mental: How MLB Players Have Embraced Psychology to Manage High Stress," *Sporting News*, April 30, 2018. www.sportingnews.com.

32. Quoted in Wyllys, "Going Mental: How MLB Players Have Embraced Psychology to Manage High Stress."

33. Quoted in Jon Robinson, "Albert Pujols Interview," *IGN*, May 19, 2006. www.ign.com.

CHAPTER FOUR: WHAT DOES IT TAKE TO MOVE TO THE NEXT LEVEL?

34. Quoted in Spenser Davis, "Oklahoma QB Kyler Murray Officially Chooses Football over Baseball: 'I Was Raised to Play QB,'" *Dallas Morning News*, February 11, 2019. https://dallasnews.com.

35. Quoted in Patrick Hayes, "Interview: Curtis Granderson Makes an Appearance at Genesee Valley Auto Mall in Flint Township," *MLive*, August 29, 2008. www.mlive.com.

36. Quoted in Steven Pivovar, "Avoiding Complacency One Goal of Fall Practices for Creighton Baseball," *Omaha World-Herald*, September 12, 2015. www.omaha.com.

37. Quoted in Emily Adams, "Senior Starter Discusses Growth with Baseball Team," *Ithacan*, April 8, 2019. https://theithacan.org.

38. Evan Grant, "Texas Rangers Second Baseman Rougned Odor on Demotion: 'I Was Not Like Me,'" *Dallas Morning News*, May 12, 2015. https://dallasnews.com.

39. Quoted in Mike DiGiovanna, "Rise of Longoria Matches the Rays," *Los Angeles Times*, October 16, 2008. www.latimes.com.

FOR FURTHER RESEARCH

BOOKS

Editors of Baseball America, *Baseball America 2019 Almanac*. Durham, NC: Baseball America, 2019.

Stuart A. Kallen, *Careers If You Like Sports*. San Diego, CA: ReferencePoint Press, 2018.

Brian Kenny, *Ahead of the Curve: Inside the Baseball Revolution*. New York: Simon & Schuster, 2017.

Keith Law, *Smart Baseball: The Story Behind the Old Stats That Are Ruining the Game, the New Ones That Are Running It, and the Right Way to Think about Baseball.* New York: William Morrow, 2017.

Nel Yomtov, *The Belles of Baseball: The All-American Girls Professional Baseball League*. Minneapolis, MN: Abdo Publishing, 2017.

INTERNET SOURCES

John Cissik, "Get Stronger in the Off-Season with This 16-Week Baseball Training Program," *STACK*, September 1, 2018. www.stack.com.

Dave Holt, "Travel Baseball vs. Rec Ball. Baseball Parents Wonder What to Do?" *Coach and Play Baseball*, n.d. www.coachandplaybaseball.com.

Joe Lopez, "Hydration Tips for a Long Baseball Season," *STACK*, March 28, 2012. www.stack.com.

Phil Tognetti, "Basic Baseball Nutrition," *The Full Windup*, n.d. www.fullwindup.com.

WEBSITES

Bleacher Report

https://bleacherreport.com

This sports website includes baseball news with current happenings, updates to players, and team information. It provides light reading and recent tweets about players and teams.

Major League Baseball

www.mlb.com

The official website of MLB includes a variety of information about players, teams, and statistics. The site is searchable by players, positions, teams, and leagues.

Minor League Baseball

www.milb.com

The official website for the MLB's minor league contains news articles, standings, and schedules.

INDEX

IMAGE CREDITS

Cover: © bmcent1/iStockphoto
5: © Chris Carlson/AP Images
7: © Gino Santa Maria/Shutterstock Images
8: © Bill Florence/Shutterstock Images
11: © tammykayphoto/Shutterstock Images
14: © sportpoint/Shutterstock Images
16: © 4 PM production/Shutterstock Images
18: © Andrey_Popov/Shutterstock Images
21: © Keeton Gale/Shutterstock Images
23: © Jamie Roach/Shutterstock Images
25: © Mike Groll/AP Images
31: © Dennis Ku/Shutterstock Images
34: © Flavio Beltran/Shutterstock Images
37: © Kiian Oksana/Shutterstock Images
40: © tammykayphoto/Shutterstock Images
43: © MTaira/Shutterstock Images
46: © sirtravelalot/Shutterstock Images
49: © Frank Romeo/Shutterstock Images
51: © Red Line Editorial
52: © Eric Broder Van Dyke/Shutterstock Images
55: © a katz/Shutterstock Images
58: © Cynthia Farmer/Shutterstock Images
60: © Martha Irvine/AP Images
62: © Chris Minor/Shutterstock Images
65: © Todd Yates/Corpus Christi Caller-Times/AP Images

ABOUT THE AUTHOR

Shirley Duke is a longtime baseball fan. She grew up watching the Texas Rangers baseball team and continued to do so with her husband and sons over the years. In fact, many summer vacations centered on seeing as many baseball stadiums and games as possible. She is a former science teacher and has written sixty-five nonfiction books for young people. She and her husband now live in the Jemez Mountains of New Mexico.